T0129317

# Love Poems I've Always Wanted to Hide

Lyric Perez

authorHOUSE®

*AuthorHouse™*
*1663 Liberty Drive*
*Bloomington, IN 47403*
*www.authorhouse.com*
*Phone: 1 (800) 839-8640*

*Published by AuthorHouse   06/11/2018*

*ISBN: 978-1-5462-4607-7 (sc)*
*ISBN: 978-1-5462-4606-0 (e)*

*To the Universe, Spirit, The Creator, Love*

To my loving and supportive parents, my beautiful and loving sisters, and my amazing nephew. To my extended family & close friends, you are family to me and inspire me. Thank you for sharing your unconditional love.

To the people who love me unconditionally, practiced unconditional love with me, have loved me, and those who will love me unconditionally in the future.

To inspirational poets who remind me what ambition is, and inspiring me to be creatively vulnerable, giving me the courage to invest in myself. This book is an inspired contribution to self, partly, because of you.

To you, the reader, for picking up this book out of curiosity, for supporting the thought of what I have to say, in a book filled with excerpts, prose, and poems. I appreciate your support and I hope you have been led by your intuition to purchase this and gain some knowledge from my experiences.

*"The Words of his mouth were smoother than butter, but war was in his heart: his words were softer than oil, yet were they drawn swords."*
**- Psalms 55:21 KJV**

# Contents

# Introduction

## My Spiritual search for Love

It wasn't until I was 25 years old that I started questioning myself about the relationships I've experienced. At 25 years old, I ended a relationship that made me question my worth and self respect. When I chose to leave, I felt free, light even. As if I just saved my own life.

I picked up a book that taught me what love was. Love wasn't about loving another more than yourself or doing all you can to make another person happy. Love was meant to start with self. By loving yourself wholeheartedly and completely, you become honest with yourself about any situation you put yourself in.

It wasn't until 4 years after learning this that I also learned; no one can break your heart if you love yourself. I realized that I was always trying to love and nurture someone's life more than my own. Settling became the norm because I rationalized that no one was perfect so I practiced loving others before being honest with myself.

I loved partnership (I still do), but moreover I loved connection. I cherished it. I loved sharing lives. Albeit exciting, I understood that I needed to be honest with myself regarding whose life I was sharing mine with. Time isn't real but it makes its contributions to our lives. Best to use our time wisely for it is here for us to enjoy. Why spend it with people who disrespect you and put you down because they don't feel great about themselves?

Trying to figure out who we are plays a major role in which direction we choose to go in. Knowing what we want is another pivotal factor that aligns directly with our intentions. If our intention isn't clear, we have a tendency to choose the wrong things. Every day we should ask ourselves those two questions: Who am I and what do I want?

# Preface

"Why hide?" I asked myself one morning. I finally felt the need to no longer fear judgment. I want to be completely vulnerable. Isn't that what poetry is? Complete vulnerability? Just written metaphoric truth of emotion between the writers' soul and its piece of paper?

One thing I love about being a poet is that when you share your work with others, almost always does someone feel inspired and grateful that they can relate to that same emotion. Someone once told me, "Thank you. That was amazing. I feel the same way but I could never express myself that way." What I have learned from others is that some people are better communicators than others. It has nothing to do with women vs. men.

Poetry is for everyone, the expressers and the doers. Words have power and the only way to understand oneself is by letting your thoughts out. Sharing your truth. Even if you judge your own truth, share it. I can guarantee someone has felt, feels, and has experienced the same emotions and situations you have. Some people may even experience worse.

There is healing in being truthful with yourself. Being gentle with yourself in a non judgmental way is the practice of unconditional self love. In turn, we learn how to love truly and we are then able to share that love and joy with others. No more hiding. It's okay to be honest. My past and present emotions are safe to share.

Emotions – the etymology of emotions are that of a movement. The energy of motion. They come to pass and they change constantly. There's nothing wrong with that. Now that I have grown spiritually, I am practicing courage, unconditional love for myself, and my love of poetry to share with those who also have a love for poetry.

Thank you for allowing me to share with you. I appreciate you and hope you will take some peace and courage with you too.

Be vulnerable. Embrace it. Embrace your truth.

# *My turn to be vulnerable —*

*I* was born in Queens, New York. Ever since I was as little girl, I searched for love. There was something about hugs and kisses that made everything about my experience feel secure and limitless. I had a huge imagination and my mom worked quite often. I played with my older sister, six years my senior. When we were very young we made cars out of cardboard boxes, played with Barbie Dolls and I watched her grow quickly into different phases of adolescence as she gave me lessons on dancing, dressing well, how to change hairstyles, and how I should take care of myself.

I often felt empty, not having the home of two parents. My mother often tired from her workload as a NYC Paramedic, always took to her bed after a hard days work. So instead, I looked towards the world trying to master my image while playing manhunt on apartment building rooftops and hanging out with the local kids from my neighborhood on street corners and an area we called, "The Pit", a generally long area of concrete in between apartment buildings that led to a backyard of gated grass.

I often saw people attempt to fall in love around me. I witnessed a heartbroken woman when I was 8 years old and remember thinking to myself why a woman would cry about breaking up with a boyfriend. Of course, I knew nothing about desperate love but immediately took on the trait that one must be sad when they are no longer with someone they consider a boyfriend. So I made sure I cried when my elementary sweetheart broke up with me, and then again when my boyfriend called it quits when I was 14 years old, and then again when I was 16 years old and then again at 23, and again at 25, and again. I didn't cry because I felt rejected, many of the decisions of separation was my own. I cried because I knew things were going to change and I have to start all over again with someone else and potentially go through another split again some day.

I clung onto the desire of stability. I constantly yearned for a man to love me with the upmost desires to make me happy. I've come to understand that the only way someone could love you properly is if they love themselves, responsible for their life choices, disciplined in areas that matter most, and are content with themselves looking to share happiness with someone else. Overtime I've learned that love is respect and has no expectations. That in order to love oneself before loving someone else, they are honest about the path they want to take, the lifestyle they want to have, and the appreciation they have for their family even though they may not agree with everyone.

I am still on the path of self-love. I practice loving myself with the reminder that I am unable to settle for a love that is unkept and misunderstood. I practice loving myself and nurture the delicate wounds that I've experienced, in hopes that I will always attract healthy love.

No matter how many failed relationships I've had, let me rephrase; No matter how many times I took a risk to fall in love and be in a committed relationship, I've learned to not be in fear about the next one to come. A relationship that does not work out will only be as painful as you allow it. Nothing should be more fulfilling then knowing you are no longer wasting your time with someone who is unable and/or unwilling to give you what you need or vice versa. After all, everyone deserves happiness the way they deem fit. Leaving a relationship that is no longer fitting for you should have you feeling free and excited. You are now closer to meeting a partner who is best for you; someone you can spend the rest of your life with if you choose.

Another reason to be free of fear is because no one deserves your old baggage. It is important to stay focused on taking care of yourself, enjoying your friends, making new ones, and living a happy life. It is imperative to keep your good energy because that is the energy you will attract.

And that's what I've learned, what I try to remember, and what I continue to understand in order to get over the desperation of thinking an unfit relationship is worth settling for.

These poems are a part of my experience with loves journey from adolescence to adulthood. It took me a long time to have the audacity to put this out, but here it is.

# When Things Begin — We Cling

Love feels so good you naturally want to feel it constantly.
It is the remedy to all pain and suffering.
To be loved without asking for it,
to experience unrequited love,
can make us create an attachment to it.

How can we love and be detached?
How can we be attentive and be detached?
How can we be devoted and be detached?

# Infatuate Me Permanently

I am love,
So filled,
It pours out of my eyelids when I am overwhelmed,
my mouth when I desire,
and my body when chemistry matches mine.
I am love
Habitually addicted
In permanent infatuations
For the moment and each moment you've gone missing.
I become detached
Because I can't lose me
Ego
It's confusing

# Let's Meet Again

A love based on spirit moves differently
Spiritual things may not allow much room for permanence
Since we are stardust formed into souls who journey
We need to turn supernova eventually

Forever is simply a word for infinite.
And infinitely my love will be with you

I will visit you each lifetime
Searching for your truth during each journey your soul goes on

# Nothing Really Matters

We are nothing but everything at the same time.

Encompassing energy that communes with other energies.
Therefore, the only way we can be active is through our communication.
Communicating through every five sense there is.
Even with the spirits, we achieve this

You cannot determine love, but rather know that You Are Love, and although your mind may pull you out of expressing it to certain energies, you indeed can share it with whomever or whatever you choose simultaneously.

Love can never be in possession of anything physical. It just is.

And one who doesn't love or has a hard time loving oneself should never take up your loving energy

For it is precious and makes us whole, guiding us to all that we seek

Be love, love yourself, and never give that up.

# Bedtime

I hide,
head under the covers,
to conceal sad thoughts

My firm pillows
Saturated by sweat
From distress

Isn't it so silly?
You,
cling to companionship

Clinging out of necessity
Necessarily filling your voids of brokenness
While breaking my heart

Every year skips summer
And like clockwork
Spring, autumn,
Winter's the longest

And just like that
I awake
Head over covers
And stare you in the face

# When Things Fall Apart

I have always made the choice of letting someone go. Regardless of how much I wanted to believe the person I chose to love was the one that was going to grow with me. One thing I have learned in my adult life is that your intuition is your truth. It tells you all you need to know about the life you are choosing. It is your SOUL speaking to you, telling you what it needs. The more you choose to ignore it, the more memories you create before you finally decide to live the life you truly desire. Not everyone is for you and that is okay. No matter how scary it is - it is your choice to move along with your life as you see fit. The more self-love you have, the less you allow anything less than love.

# Midnight Train

Peaceful,
Awake

All else rests,
Eyes softly closed for the road
Each journey,
Unique
But my journey,
Preeminent
Because my journey,
Involves you

The squeaking of train tracks in an upright seat never felt more comfortable

# Unbalanced

$\mathcal{I}$ wish I knew what perfection was
To embody appreciation at its highest point
To love intensely everyday without a moment of sadness, fear, or boredom,
Without wonderment of where the balance is
No yin and yang
Everyday perfection
Dew,
No rain,
Then sunshine,
Repeating itself in 60 to 85 degree weather with occasional bouts of snow
Everyone has a 5 bedroom home to live in
Choice of house, mansion, or apartment living

The moon,
Always full without the tides being pulled
All of us in tune with our spiritual man
Acknowledging our body is spirits' opportunity to cease the day until our
time is up
Marriage becomes a fearless blessing
Partnership becomes miraculous

I wish I knew what perfection was
To embody appreciation at its highest point
To love intensely everyday without a moment of sadness, fear, or boredom,
Without wonderment of where the balance is
No yin and yang
Everyday perfection
Dew,
No rain,
Then sunshine

# Fragmented

I found you alone with wings
Standing there
Your appetite to fly was that of a homeless child,
Confused,
Starved,
With infinite solutions
But with a belly full of fear that nothing will get solved
The anatomy of you,
Broken
Fractured wing and torn feathers
Ashamed,
You were unable to soar

Safe to say fractures heal too
And feathers do grow back
And look at you
Just look...

Now

Fly

You

How

At

# Who Wants to Wishfully Think

Jump behind the stars we've watched & wished upon
Jump into ditches we've tried to avoid
Sing forever, at the top of your lungs of songs we've hated
Tie me up in your memories where I can live forever
Your worst fears of failure live in the grating of your sawed away teeth
Breathe hard like an out of shape senior citizen with emphysema,
The sweat can't cool you down
There's no such thing as Beauty
Yet you fear the Beautiful anyway
For you,
Love is an old fable told and trust is something only art can imitate

## Our Favorite Toy

An etch a sketch romance of sorts
Scratches on the screen
Knobs gritty & grey
Shaken aluminum powder becomes a melody
Until the stylus breaks

# Live In The Moment

---

*H*ave faith - see it come to life
Be patient with the universe - the plan is preparing itself

Don't spend time sulking spend time living

Enjoy life - although you don't have what you desire immediately think about the things you are grateful for. Things you are blessed with. You will find that instead of complaining and feeling down you are happy with the things you already have. Don't spend time sulking. Spend time living.

Unbeknownst to you, you still have experiences to go through, things to achieve before achieving your absolute goal. Which by the way, your goals never end.

You'll find when you're not obsessed with the absolute goal; you'll enjoy your journey day by day. I'm not saying forget about your goal, I'm saying enjoy your process getting there.

# Untitled

We lie to protect ourselves.
And then we lie to ourselves.
But that,
Is dangerous

# Nostalgic

Enigmatic privacy of a memory
Etched in emotions of roadways, seasons, Kleenex tissues, & old songs
Third loves feel like first loves
Holding hands in public and massaging feet on park benches
Made the serotonin levels high
On nights like this,
Old loves are remembered
Despite misery,
Or discouraging words that flutter off of beautiful lips,
Prying eyes that once invaded privacy,
Of uncommitted commitments
Fears of teenage wedding vows in front of an alter made of yard trees
The love never dies
The roots were never pulled
So every spring a garden of roses grow with the sharpest of thorns
Reminding them what beauty looked like,

Although it hurt like hell

# Gardener

He saw his reflection in me
The innocent part of him
The determination of fasting for 40 days and 40 nights
Just to get to the soul of me
Just to get to the soul of him

Green leaves turned brown can never make their way back onto the branches
So he waters his roots
Praying for the sunlight

He knows

He internalizes

The biggest tree doesn't grow over night

# Fiction

Such a fabulous life

Confusion tickles the heart,
Burrows it's way back into the mind,
Releases itself from the eyes

Such a temporary life

Humility & ego fight to the death,
Slipping it's way into the tone of voice,
Turning ones vocabulary into the perfect contrition

We tuck our heads under the covers
Afraid of a hug,
Un-love-able,
We all fear what could be unconditional

Too bad,
What a pity,
No one ever told you,
Not only do monsters not exist,
But you definitely won't find their skeletons in any closet.

# Soul-full

Such a beautiful soul of a man, so in touch with the vibration of the Universe's design
The creation of what we should be
To be that,
This year, this generation,
I'm floored,
By the make up of your design

Such a beautiful soul of a man, so in touch with the discipline of his birthright
So in tuned to a purposeful life
Guiding others to live freely,
As a spirit should be,
I'm floored,
By the make up of your design

Such a beautiful soul of a man, so in touch with his respect for the womb
So patient in your ambition
Women seek a soul like you for years, hoping that you seek them
Don't know who would have given up on your desires to love wholeheartedly
Silly them,
Lucky me,
To be admired by such a soul,
Such a beautiful soul of a man,
Like yours

# Abort

Yes,
I felt as if my spirit was pulled from my soul when we departed each other
My womb became void,
Yet again,
Defeated,
By a young woman's decision to surgically remove her undeveloped fetus

It was you,
No longer growing within me
Death inside of me
A still born of love

Attempts, you were persistent to make
But I had cysts in my ovaries for you
What a feeling it is,
To let go and break free

So now I sing funeral songs to my memories
I sing freedom songs to my future
And I sing love-
Love,
Love,
Let's get it right this time,
At all times
But this time,
Not with you

*Passion*

_____

$\mathcal{F}$it me like a glove
See the world for what it isn't
Develop giggles inside of my womb
Pitter-patter kisses on my back
Savor my fingertips with your taste buds
Graze my collarbone with the tip of your lips
Honor me with your hands
Create offerings to my creation
I will season our world with beautiful children
Planting each seed for the glory of us
Healing hearts with knowledge and wisdom for growth
Come,
Create with me, Creator

# Three Haikus

Oh the Joy in Me
My heart's still, my Soul's smiling
Oh the Joy in Us

Color me Purple
Make Love to me Pastel Blue
Passion's Red in your heart

Mmmmmmm, wait, not too hard
Great, now I have a hickey
Thank you very much

# False Advertising

Your broken past of un-forgetfulness
The terror in your romantic future
You became a gallon of milk
Useful, spoiled then wasted
A rumor in a tall tale magazine
A fairytale with a bullshit ending
You are the epitome of a broken promise, a hopeless dream, and a made up God
An awful magician's mistake during an illusion in front of thousands of people
Your imagery was made up of cubic zirconium
Worth less than what it imitates
Absent dynasty of ruthless talk
You are worse than a politician's empty promises
You are fast food to a toddler
A gangster rap song to a Christians ears
A broken classic record
A monotone teacher
A goldfish swimming next to a Clown Loach
An annoying melody
Alcohol poisoning to a 15 year old
You are brainwashing Disney Stories to youthful innocent girls
Full of disappointment and deceit
The purpose of trick or treating on Halloween
European brainwash
Bitterness on the tongue from Coptis root
Credited Debt in the matrix of our government
You appeal to your audience a delightful entity
Baptized in the waters of the Nile

Better than a Gas sale on pay day
You are every type of vaccination
Man made drug
Perpetrating toxins that violently touch DNA
An airbrushed blemish
A neatly piled clutter
A carefully thought out Advertisement
To sway the minds of every silly consumer

# Without The Use of Foul Language

I closed the book on us without desire of reading the sequel
You were my equal
A treacherous poison intertwined with the finest tobacco
You were the duplicate of an admired painting sold on Ebay for 10 dollars
Your beauty,
Suppressed
By your imitation of the finest textured paint

I threw away the soul of you this morning
Vacuuming the dust bunnies our arguments left behind
Our photographs,
eaten by the silverfish that slithered out of the cracks of my window pane
I took the weight of my arm to smash down the hardest I could,
buried them as their legs wiggled,
Because in their bellies,
they wrought the last memory of you

# Preeminent

I let your love orchestrate the most beautiful organized sound against my brain waves and my heart beats drum

You make this world,
This life of mine,
Have purpose again
To sway my negative ideas into positive perspectives
Listening to my attractions
Then feeding them to me on a silver platter of Oh My God, he fed me the tastiest fruits,
Each one in its season
Held me like a baby, when you said each loving word to me
Your stares and smiles feed my loves effort with delight
My fears disappear like poisonous gases in the Earths Atmosphere

I tremble within my soul for you,
For your passionate kisses,
For your clenching hugs,
For your loving prayers,
For your Central Nervous Systems Attention to remember me,
Smell me,
Taste me,
And hear me forever in your sleep

You embody me
Draw me out in sketches of beautiful memories
Oil Pastels so slick it easily slid my make up with each divine contour
All can tell you've been there before
Memorize me like Scripture

Coloring in my pupils,
Future is Us
Inhaled my spirit
And exhaled slow
You breathe me so I can be within You
You taste me so I can be a part of You
And we become great together
Minds alike so thinking becomes exciting
Spiritual reverence for each other's souls we go deeper than this world
Intellectually fitting
My Provider has uplifted me again
This puzzle is not so confusing
I am not piecing it alone
My artist and creator
Paint me colors so earth toned
I adhere to your embrace
My melodic musician
I am your composition
So,
I will continue to let your love orchestrate the most beautiful organized
sound against my brain waves and my heart beats drum
Because you and I
Are a perfect Masterpiece

# Retrograde

You inspire me to rip away my skin so you can see the inside of me
A catastrophic threat of the worlds end so it can scare you into admitting the way you feel for me
Why don't you just drape me with religious cloth and watch me get baptized in loves name so I can be born again
and again,
and again
If only for a moment of cancelling out your fear and judgment calls
To escape this programmed culture,
for just a little bit, without telling a soul
Because the beer only gets denser
The men become balder
And Ego
That sun of a bitch, is an addict
Always wanting to be fed
Clinging onto the teat and never letting go
Plan B becomes plan A meanwhile you're afraid of Plan C
So we are armored to a tee
Ready for loves battle
Introduced ourselves betrayed 1 and betrayed 2
Kiss me then devour my soul with aggression because of your doubt and curiosity
What would this world be like if a woman had a heart of gold?
Your vision of faithfulness like remnants of faded chalk
Loyalty
A challenge to your testosterone
You imagine if we all were vulnerable,
Love would be a lie,
A painful thief in the night

Well, I invite you to
Read me like an open book
Slowly skim through my highlighted quotes
Although my binding is old and has shed many pages,
They remain in the cover
It may appear worn
But the lessons remain
I am made from the earth's debris
I anticipate oxygen, gentle touches, and love from my surroundings
Come,
Read me,
Humans are God's experiment gone awry
And here we are,
Making it worse

## Monotony is his blind eye

Leave me behind like wet mops and dusty brooms
As your rough hands hang artillery for a weeks salary
Tired,
Bored,
Sweaty,
Hungry,
Hunting for attention because you're
Tired,
Bored,
Sweaty,
Hungry
Starving,
Thirsty,
Craving,
For more

# Good Luck

Good Luck with your tomorrow
With your empty chest
With your dissatisfaction of a woman who
Paraded and danced along your collar bone although,
You were flawed
And insecure

Good Luck with your dreams
with your subconscious desire for me
with every nightmare you wake up from
shivering and wondering
How could you have let me slip away from your fingertips that weren't
sticky enough to hold on to me?

Good Luck with your search
with your hiding behind digital curtains
with your typo'd love letters to strangers
ducking underneath your shyness and lack of confidence
catching up with former lovers just to feel embraced

Good Luck with your House
with the remembrance of who made it a home
with the times you will shed a tear while doing a chore I once took pride in
finding my old love letters in hidden places
remembering what a romantic woman I was

Good Luck with Your Heart
with the soul of your laziness
with your mind and your ambition

See, unconditional lovers have a way of forgiving
We don't take mistakes personally
It's never been me,
It's always been you.

All My Best,

Good Luck

## Hole

Always blaming the rabbit for his tardiness
When it was you who was always late & out of your mind

# Make Up Your Mind

We are good at being at odds
Small children trying to grow up
and be teachers
Husband and Wife isn't easy
Bachelor and Bachelorette is all we've known
We've perfected the art in serial dating
Serious is confusing

Seriously,
I'm confused

# Music, My Love For It

I wish my words could play a harmony for you
The beat would be the pulse of your veins,
Pumping blood to your heart
A sound proof room with studio equipment demanding your private attention
Quiet
Aware
Peace-full
Loving the words I say
Admiring them
Guess this paper and your room will do

*Extension*

It's not easy
Choosing a total stranger
To welcome into your life
As family
To blend DNA
To trust
To slumber with every night you close your eyes
To be confident they will take care of your offspring with unconditional
love
To nurture
To pray for
To love
To share hard earned income with
To buy a home together
To cook for
To be vulnerable to
To be honest
To fear to lose
To celebrate every season with
To choose a stranger
Turning them into family
That's the miracle of love
That's magic
To extend ourselves
We are all we have, family

# Childlike

*I* wonder if being in love is easier when we are younger.
All that time on our hands and not many financial worries
Makes me wonder,
If we are to be happy, free adults, then certainly,
Our loving would be deeper.
Perhaps freedom is the ultimate condition for happiness.

# Sense Memory

Broken Hearts so vivid
Creatures of habit
Habits never loved me
Neither did the darkness in you
Nor did it recognize what your value was
Because if it did,
You'd take care of you
By taking care of Me

# Goals

Let's play in sunsets together
Where we share one common goal
Family and a life of humble spontaneity
Kiss me on my forehead without me having to ask kind of man
Fearless and hopeful
Never jealous
Only emulating confidence
A real man who inspires, supports, and uplifts
One who would never put me down but rather lift me up because he feels the same way about himself
Melody
Warm weather
Live Instrumentation
Planes
Holidays
Lazy Sundays
Home cooked meals
Poetry
Laughing from our guts
Divine lovemaking
Breakfast for two
Cuddling my dog like she is yours
Just loving

# Reverse

He is the King of Swords in reverse
The Hangman
The Hermit
The Queen of Cups
Upside down,
you'd rather be,
than making this life beautiful
here
with me

*It's like a shot to the heart*
*But I'm bullet proof there*

*Fuck a scar,*
*You can never cut me that deep*

# Colorless

I was faded like watercolors
Moving through this sphere
Like the wind as it tossed me
Right into you
Faded but beautiful
I thought I was designed to give you a more delicate color
Until you turned me black and white

*He hurt me*
*And now it hurts him*

# Murderer

One day
I'm not going to be here anymore
And you threw me away
Before my time was up

# No Expectations

Are you drifting away?
I no longer know what to expect with you
Maybe I wouldn't have to talk to psychics to figure out the answers you
can simply provide me with
With your lying ass

# Liar

Honesty is freeing
Thank you for freeing me.

# Dungeons

It was claustrophobic there
But the promise was spacious, vibrant, and breathtaking
You hid behind your parading words
Wore your wings well but took them off when I wasn't around
Promises became popular
As others believed you could fly too
But once I saw them crooked, falling off your back, I flew away instead
Tears don't fall down to his cheeks
I'm a believer of this

What he tries to master is his mind

Focused on Federal Reserve notes
And the proud passion of living a life of accomplishments through his work

He leaves the sorrows for tomorrow
So in solitude he can cry out with dry tears
Reliving his past through pictures
Wishing he could speak up
But instead he swallows his pride
To feel alive
As a man should
Be tough
As a man should
Be emotionless
As a man should
What a life worth living he convinces himself

# Coerced

Forced myself to love you
Because I didn't like you anymore
Still not sure if it was worth it
I would've rather loved myself completely instead

## Sex with You

Feel the depths of me
Relieving me from fear
Bring me closer to God
God,
You feel good

# Malcolm

Chemistry
You must be magic
I can't find my scars

# Settling For Chemistry

I allow you to keep me in rotation
When I don't want to rotate you
Stars stay still until they die
But not you and I
We are like the Earth
Constantly rotating
So please,
Continue

# West 138th Street

We were born in Harlem
Between thin walls
Narrow hallways
And High Ceilings
Eyes piercing
Wide
Open
Creative energy
You flowed to me
Charmer with depth
Your touches were hypnotizing
Conversations
Delectable
Confidence & Appetite for me
Enchanting
Such a shame
The depth of such emotions
Can get in the way

The wall of China has nothing on mine

I've been waiting in your wings
Dying to take flight
Spending years at a time
Ending every beginning
Waiting for every beginning to turn into forever

I only make love for the experience
When the energy feels right
But truthfully
I am tired of giving away pieces of me
For I am sacred,
Exclusive,
And you should be so lucky
That I gave you this pie

I told him I don't like to play games
As he turned every page of me
trying to solve a puzzle

# The Secret

I scratch my own back
I comb my own hair, put it up and style it nice
I run my own bath water, wash myself gently
I dance alone like no one is watching
I make my own bed, fluff my own pillows
I tuck myself in after a long day
I remind myself how beautiful I am
I love with passion
I read to myself
I cook healthy meals with flavor so I can live well
I am patient with myself when I find I'm not gentle enough
I sing songs aloud
I scratch my own back, rub my own shoulders
I practice
A lot
Of loving
Me
So I know what standards to set
For when you walk into my life

# Botanica

It's sorcery
What you did to me
Burning candles in the living room
Counting beads in your prayers prose
We are close,
Closer to the gods
When we make love
Blowing cigar smoke
To see futures past
Past the currents
Of your energy
I see the you in me
The you in me
The eulogy for you,
in me,
won't allow me to recover
The potion's dense
This dream intense
I'm way deeper than your Lover

# Time Travel

In time,
everything aligns

Like what we have right now
Right now
What we have
Right now

Come back again
in the future
Right now

I'll wait for you
Right now

I have no future
Right now

We are forever ending
Right now

Always beginning
Right now

I'm not pretending
Right now

# Flow – Float – Let Go

It is a challenging thing, maybe the most difficult for me,
To love without fear
That I may lose it

Knowing that love is as self-less as it is full of self.
But it is self-less most of all.
It's a magical energy, love.

Real love can become a struggle of sorts.
Within the duality of the egoic mind
We, the ones who possess so many things in the material world
Make a habit of such.

Real love, like the metaphor of Love is God, God is Love,
Has to be achieved through ones own spirit, ones own soul
Can love really be lost?
Where will it go?
Is God lost?
Can you Lose God?

When the Love is Real,
it has nowhere to go.
It exists, it thrives, it heals, it understands.
It understands that our journeys are different
It understands that we can't all be the same
Doing the same thing,
At the same place at the same time

We vary,
Moving wavelengths
Towards each other,
Current-ly
Temporarily
Sometimes anyway

We are all love,
Let's just call each other love

Love, you are never lost
Even when your flesh gives away to its immortality

Love, you will never be bereaved
Even when the sun sets and arises somewhere else

Love, be yourself
And understand
That other Loves need your Love too
So be sure to Love you
As you are
As they are

And I guarantee, that when you Love for Real
Like you Love You
You will never be worried about Losing Love
Because Love can't lose you

# Over Lover

Pardon me
If I squeeze you too tight
At night
In the morning
Or dawn

Pardon me
For stealing kisses randomly
For reasons like,
Time may be up soon
And I don't wanna leave you
But I know everything comes to an end

So Starshine,
Let's not pretend
We were meant to be friends
And not lovers
Under the covers
Over the sheets
On floors
And then some

Remind me where you came from

Local alien,
Conundrum

Pardon me
if I wake up early most mornings
to make your favorite breakfast
& worship your body
before the day starts anew
but what is one to do?

Look at you

# Come Again

Sing me ballads
of love songs across my neck with your lips
your breath in my ears
your touch on my thighs
alive
im awake
and dying at the same time
into your chest
is where I belong.

# Loving of the Self Is The Ultimate Recipe

I remember there was a time that I would treat courting like a game
That caught up to me until I learned how to completely love myself
Now I no longer desperately try to make a man see why they should love me
I love me. I know my offerings.
Now, if there is something I see, I let go of any fantasy.
I know what I want.

## Storyteller

I don't believe in folklore
Fairytales, fables, or nursery rhymes
I know the song and dance
All too well
I know every line
Like the lines in my palms

# Bad Magician

I saw what you did there, silly

# Apologetic

I'm tired of hearing whispers of I love you as I am dying

It's a deafening death,
when the one you adore,
thinks they'd prefer someone prettier,

They mustn't recognize
the God in you

Crucified

Static

I'm just a dusty exhibit
In his museum of muses
For I'm not the only one he chooses

# Knowing the Difference

*L*ife's too precious to care about you giving your dick away
to loose women who vibrate at a low frequency.

That's your prerogative. Not mine.

I'm the one that says I love you and I miss you.
You're the one who tells me you miss my *face* and
you'd *f u c k* me forever.

# The Power of Words

---

$\mathcal{I}$ was reading Bell Hooks and the way we speak about sex and how we use the term fucking which means to cheat or hurt a person. The intent behind the word "fuck" is a threat of violence. We think this is normal; "Pain is love". We go about disrespecting ourselves; not loving ourselves because we *think* it is normal. We are what we think, we create what we think, and here we are... thinkers, creators, and seekers of love, divided.

# Keep it Real

Choking in the pit of my stomach
Your selective honesty continues to succeed although I gave you all the secrets to this relationships success.
So you choke me
Instead of giving me air

Don't you ever get tired of causing my tears?

# Isadora

Always pregnant,
Always giving birth
Seeds forever coming to fruition
Differently than planned
No handbook
Just choices & lessons
Becoming footprints left behind
For my children
That have gone unborn
Future children
Seems so futuristic
Like flying cars with no traffic lights

I was born in a desert of family-less generations
A nation is nothing to stand by
Mothers day forgotten due to clout
Family is further
birds leaving nests behind without saying the right words
hopefully I'll boomerang

# Fuck Hiding

---

If you want to be free, you need to be free of your own fears
When you are afraid, you stifle yourself.
Unmoving. Stuck.
Quiver and move on. What you feel, everyone else has felt or is feeling now.
Control your wave length and what you welcome into your life by being
the energy & making wise choices that will make your journey what you
want it to be. When I wanted to hide these poems, I wanted to hide myself.
But that, hiding, is just silly.

Printed in the United States
By Bookmasters